T0142672

"BELLA BECOMES A POODLE"

Deborah Egan

To order additional copies of this book, contact:
Xlibris
844-714-8691
www.Xlibris.com
Orders@Xlibris.com

ISBN: Softcover   979-8-3694-1563-4
         Hardcover   979-8-3694-1562-7
         EBook   979-8-3694-1561-0

Library of Congress Control Number: 2024902317

Print information available on the last page

Rev. date: 02/20/2024

This book is dedicated to my granddaughter Genevieve, who has a tireless willingness to bring joy to others through her smiles and goodwill of heart, and my loving husband, Bill, who endlessly encourages me to persevere with patience in all things, especially the completion of this first book.

About The Author

Deborah Egan was a stay-at-home mother of four. She attended two years of college and discovered her love for writing and the gratification of making people laugh. Blessed with a husband, children, grandchildren, and the ability to travel, she now lives in North Carolina.

About The Illustrator

Genevieve McVaugh is ten years old and began illustrating for her grandmother when she was in the fourth grade. She was selected as the 2023 contest winner for her art work.

"BELLA BECOMES A POODLE"

Story by
Deborah Egan

Illustrations by
Genevieve McVaugh

Just about three months had passed since the fluffy poof of a puppy entered the big world. Bouncing and pouncing was a favorite pastime of the yet-to-be-discovered, playful little "puff-of-a-luff" brown pup.

In just two short weeks, Lynn the groomer would begin to accustom young Bella to getting trimmed up, soaking in a nice warm bath, and having a gentle blow-drying to keep her looking beautiful.

It was a bright, sunny January morning, and the special day had arrived! At just fourteen weeks old, Bella was lifted with love from the car, wrapped in her warm mom's arms with a cute pink leash attached to her dainty little purple collar, and carried to what would later become known as her "Spa Day." Although she had no idea what lay ahead, she sensed it was something new and special.

Lynn excitedly greeted Bella and her parents at the door with a bountiful smile, as the furry puppy jostled about in the salon. "She'll be fine," Lynn said softly. "I'll give you a call when she's ready to be picked up."

"Thank you, Lynn," said Bella's mom. "Just a simple little trim will be perfect!"

A few hours passed, and the call came that petite Bella was all beautified and ready for pick-up. "She looks great!" exclaimed Bella's mom.

Time flew by swiftly, and sure enough, two months later, it was spring and once again time for the growing young dog to go for her next tidying-up day.

"Hi Bella!" exclaimed Lynn. "What are we going to do today? Would you like me to try trimming Bella's face to let you see a little more of what she could look like? After all, she is a poodle."

"Sure, go ahead. We just don't want her to be one of those poofy, froufrou poodles. Have fun!" said Bella's mom and dad.

A while later, the call came that it was time to pick up Bella. Bella's parents then discovered she had a long nose beneath all the fur that had been shaved away! It was amazing! Who would have known she could be more beautiful than before? Her short fluffy, puffy, furry nose was now shiny, skinny, chic, and soft as velvet.

Little by little, and very unintentionally, Bella's elegance was being discovered. Her mom and dad laughed, the pooch smiled, and they scheduled her next beauty visit.

Summer was upon them, and sweet girl Bella's tail was wagging, but her tongue was panting. Now she was seven months old, and her coat was growing rapidly. She was feeling the heat of the sun evermore readily. Her next appointment had arrived just in time, and the groomer was more than happy to accommodate the hot, growing puppy.

"How about we give her a pom on her tail? We can keep it on the longer side so as to not make her look too fancy, because I know you don't really want a crazy, extravagant look. We'll let her ears grow a little longer, and I'll touch up her face again and trim her a little closer so she doesn't get too hot, OK?"

Bella's mommy and daddy agreed that letting her ears grow in a little more wouldn't affect her too much with the upcoming warmer season. They handed Bella over to Lynn and stepped out the door quickly, so as not to make the excited pup too nervous. Waving good-bye to both Lynn and their beloved pet, they anxiously anticipated picking her up and having her back in their home.

After waiting nearly eight long hours and accomplishing a few errands, the cell phone gave its expected buzz and vibration. It was Lynn. Bella was ready for her chauffeur. The sun was setting quickly, and the parents of the brown puppy were looking forward to seeing their baby. Hastily grabbing the car keys, they happily drove off into the sunset toward the doggy beauty salon.

It seemed like it took forever to arrive at the puppy's spa. Darkness had set in, but nonetheless, they reached their destination. As they approached the entrance, little barks could be heard, as if Bella somehow knew she was going home.

The door was opened, and before they knew it, their fluffy canine friend was right before them. Bella's mommy and daddy were quite surprised. They hardly recognized her! Before their eyes was what looked like another dog! There she was with all her energy, wagging tail, wiggling body, and pink tongue hanging out the side of her muzzle, awaiting approval.

"Oh my gosh!" exclaimed Bella's family. "She looks so … poodley. She looks so different."

"I thought I would leave the top of her hair, be a little wild, and give her a bouffant on her head as well as the pom on her tail," groomer Lynn said quietly. "I didn't think you would mind."

Smiling and bending down to give little Miss Bella a hug of approval and love, her mom looked up with acceptance and gratitude and said to Lynn, "Well, you're right; she is a poodle, and we definitely can see that now!"

It was surely true that only with time and coming of age can true beauty be revealed.

Months passed by, totaling over a year and a half. The pup had taken multiple trips to the canine spa, and miniature Bella had grown into her full self, or at least that was what Bella's parents thought. Along with all the transformations dear Bella had undergone came the move from Pennsylvania to North Carolina. New adventures were on the horizon, one of which was finding a new groomer.

It seemed as though an angel was placed in the lives of Bella and her mommy and daddy the day they met Angela. She was a jubilant, cheerful, good ole Southerner from the quaint small town of Leland, about fifteen short minutes from Bella's new home. With Bella strutting beside them, tethered to her new florescent, flashy pink leash, all three approached Angela's home. The house was enhanced with a welcoming "Dogs Spoiled Here" sign and a white picket fence conveniently placed for all those wishing to experience "A New Doggy Look." Bella and her family excitedly entered.

"Come on in!" Bella's new stylist exclaimed with a big ole smile stretching clear across her beautiful face. The adults chatted, and inquisitive Bella was permitted to wander around her new friend's doggy salon. Bella put her nose to work and enjoyed sniffing around, getting acquainted with her new surroundings.

The time had come now to hand the fully grown sixty-four-pound canine over to her new sculptor and trust Angela's hands with all the tools she had been gifted in order to fashion a fresh creation for this big girl and give her a new look to match her new "down South" home.

"Give me just 'n hour 'n' a half," she said with her sweet Southern drawl, "and she'll be ready for pick-up. OK?"

Bella got her pats, and Mom and Dad lovingly said good-bye.

Just as timely as Angela had said, the notification popped up on the cell phone. The text message read, "Bella's ready for pick-up. Y'all can come get her."

Arriving at the garage door, Bella's parents were graciously welcomed by groomer Angela, Bella's new best bud. "Come on in, y'all!" she said excitedly. "What do y'all think?"

Bella stood there with her sparkling brown human-like eyes filled with love, as if to say thank you.

"I hope y'all don't mind. I forgot to ask you about boots," Angela said softly, looking downward.

"What do you mean?" Bella's mom asked. Bella was standing quite close, so neither one of Bella's parents had noticed.

"Look at her legs. What do y'all think? Winter's coming on, and I thought y'all would like Miss Bella to go out in style down here in the South, so I gave her some boots—some 'leg warmers'!" Angela laughed heartily.

There Bella stood, beautiful and proud with her new Southern look. All she needed was her big "down South" wide-brim hat! She had grown into a fully developed, beautiful Standard Poodle. With her full, fluffy ears; narrow, closely shaved, long, soft snout; fancy bouffant hairdo; sleekly clipped body and legs; and her new, stylish, thick, furry boots, she looked up at them all with her happy eyes and jubilant pom wagging back and forth on her tail.

The little fluff of a pup, and her parents too, had discovered that given the gift of time, maturity, and experience, all that is sometimes hidden is eventually discovered. True beauty lies deep. You only need to be patient for it to be revealed.

15

Printed in the United States
by Baker & Taylor Publisher Services